T0090517

The Pet Owner's Guide to Emergency Veterinary Care

What Every Pet Owner Should Know to Protect Themselves, Their Pet and Their Finances

George Heath BS, LATg

BALBOA.PRESS
A DIVISION OF HAY HOUSE

Balboa Press books may be ordered through booksellers or by contacting:

Balboa Press
A Division of Hay House
1663 Liberty Drive
Bloomington, IN 47403
www.balboapress.com
844-682-1282

Because of the dynamic nature of the Internet, any web addresses or
links contained in this book may have changed since publication and
may no longer be valid. The views expressed in this work are solely those
of the author and do not necessarily reflect the views of the publisher,
and the publisher hereby disclaims any responsibility for them.

The author of this book does not dispense medical advice or prescribe
the use of any technique as a form of treatment for physical, emotional,
or medical problems without the advice of a physician or veterinarian,
either directly or indirectly. The intent of the author is only to offer
information of a general nature to help you in your quest for emotional
and spiritual well-being. In the event you use any of the information
in this book for yourself, which is your constitutional right, the author
and the publisher assume no responsibility for your actions.

Any people depicted in stock imagery provided by Getty Images are
models, and such images are being used for illustrative purposes only.
Certain stock imagery © Getty Images.

Print information available on the last page.

ISBN: 979-8-7652-4293-3 (sc)
ISBN: 979-8-7652-4294-0 (e)

Balboa Press rev. date: 06/20/2023

Contents

Dedication

This, my first published book is dedicated to my Mother Jewell Consetta Shelton, who encouraged my love for animals, biology and science from a very young age and made me believe that with knowledge and hard work nothing is impossible. To my wonderful wife Pauline C Heath who endured my love for All Creatures Great and Small along with my six kids Carol, Jeremiah, Naomi, Elizabeth, Sarah and Rachel Heath. And my siblings Warren, Steven (El-Naquam Ben Isreal) Derrick, Lisha and Albert Heath. To my Lord and Savior Jesus Christ through whom all thing are possible in accordance to his will.

Galatians 2:20-21 KJV

I am crucified with Christ, nevertheless I live, yet not I but Christ liveth in me. And the life which I now live in the flesh I live by the faith of the Son of God, who loved me and who gave himself for me.

About The Author

George Heath was born and raised on the South Side of Chicago and served in the United States Army from 1977 to 1997 as Veterinary Technician and AALAS Certified

Laboratory Animal Technologist. He served as President of the Memphis Branch of AALAS, and has been published and presented at various Veterinary and Laboratory Research Conferences and Publications

AALAS: American Association for Laboratory Animal Sciences

Foreword

By Andrea Dryer

It was the 4th of July 2022 and I arrived home to find my beloved female Cane Corso named Mama, unable to stand and panting rapidly with her gums starting to turn very pale. I rushed her to the Veterinary Hospital as fast as I could with my heart pounding and hands shaking, not knowing if she would live or die. At the Vet Clinic I was told I had to pay a $2,500.00 deposit as an emergency treatment fee which I did immediately by writing a check while thinking how on earth am I going to pay other bills or how can I rob from Peter to Pay Paul or juggle other bills that must be paid but at the moment Mama was my priority. I sat there for hours, all the while sick to my stomach and shaking nervously and sobbing crying still not knowing if she would live or die as I prayed to God for help. Eventually one of the staff came to me and informed me that unless I came up with another $5,000.00 more dollars the best option was to put my baby to sleep. I was not prepared to pay another $5,000.00, a total 0f $7,500.00 but neither was I prepared to have them kill my baby as I just broke down and sobbed. Just then I called my ex-husband Steven Heath who then called his brother George Heath. Thank God George called me immediately. He told me to get some essential information like lab results, what was her temperature and then told me to press her gums and count how many seconds for the color to return, was it under 3 seconds? He then explained to me that they have no right to euthanize my dog without my permission, as their attitude was you either pay or we have to euthanize her, we can't let her leave in this condition. George suggested to have them continue to administer fluids, perform whatever treatments that she is scheduled for over the next hour and asked me to describe her temperament and attitude towards me. After all that, after three hours of treatment, Mama seemed better, and I took control of the situation. I eventually decided and informed the staff that I would be taking my beloved Mama home, period. I was then informed that the bill was $900.00, and they would eventually refund me $1,600.00 as I had gave them a check for $2,500.00. They refused to return my check in exchange for the $900.00 and I was far too upset and traumatized by the entire experience to argue, I just left with my dog and stopped payment on the check. I then gave them another check for $900.00 the next day. I took my baby home and provided around the clock tender loving care. Everyday Mama continued to improve and is in perfect health today. I wish I had found a Veterinary Service that I could trust, but in this case every fiber of my being told me I was being taken advantage of and my dog was being held hostage. I eventually found a Vet Service I could trust and now I know the warning signs George shares in this book to recognize the red flag danger signs of predatory veterinary practices. These are insights I want every pet owner to know.

Trip to Emergency Vet Clinic

A trip to the animal emergency clinic in the wee hours of the night or weekend can be a very traumatic event in the lives of pet owners, their children and their pets. It can have a very happy ending, as often is the case. A simple treatment, some tender loving care and the expertise of the emergency care Veterinarian and staff can be nothing less than miraculous. Unfortunately, wherever there is the potential to make a quick profit off the misfortunes of others, there exist professionals that will do exactly that. Many of us who are pet owners have experienced it firsthand. Hopefully, with the help of this booklet, both veteran and novice pet owners will know what to expect and how to avoid the pitfalls that can occur in animal emergency veterinary clinics.

The veterinary emergency room can be a place of extreme emotional and financial vulnerability. A place where logic and exceptional decision making skills fall apart and the (cash cow) paying public can become prime time candidates for highly profitable applications of wonderful veterinary technological advances. It is only natural, out of pure love to say, "do whatever it takes to save Fifi, I don't care what it cost." But what if the cost, as sometimes is the case, equates to days and even weeks of agonizing suffering for a pet that is going to die or even worse, condemned to live a life with no quality of life at all? This is when the gift of euthanasia can be the greatest final gift any pet owner can give his or her pet. I will tell you what some (not all) emergency medicine veterinarians will not and hopefully you can use this information as a balance and make the right decision for you, your pet and your financial wellbeing.

Veterinary Advances

Just Because They Can Doesn't Mean You Should

The majority of todays advanced large volume veterinary clinics are not the small owner operations of yesterday. Many possess extremely expensive modern in house laboratory, ultrasound and radiographic equipment along with emergency life support systems that would put some small town human clinics to shame. All these top notch technological advancements when combined with cutting edge veterinary skills and training of experienced Veterinarians and Veterinary Technicians can snatch Fifi or Fido from the jaws of death and restore him or her to a quality of life and back into the hands of a happy and grateful pet owner in a manner that is nothing less than miraculous.

It has been my experience that there are many Veterinarians that will do what is in the best interest of you and your pet, and will not take advantage of a pet's owner's love for their pet in a no win situation. Unfortunately, there are many who have been trained and groomed to initially present a financial cost or estimate that meets their minimum expense goals regardless of your pet's needs or your financial limitations. To be totally honest and realistic, we must face the fact that many large Veterinary practices are big business franchises that must pay for all those cutting edge technologies, diagnostic and medical equipment and the high cost of modern veterinary therapies they make readily available. Many Veterinarians work on salary plus commissions, that is the more you pay to keep Fifi alive, the more they make at the end of the week. The bottom line is this, while there are many that might do what is in the best interest of their patient, your beloved pet, there are others that will milk you for every penny they can justify which may not be in your or your pet's best interest. Often in emergency situations even when the prognosis is poor and the eventual treatment is unaffordable, there will be a rush to do the basics; x-rays, bloodwork, chemistry, initial intravenous therapy and treatments in order to presumably provide you with a diagnosis. The initial cost being around $500.00 for the upfront procedures (X-rays, Bloodwork, Chemistries) to 1,500.00 and more for the initial first overnight stay and hospitalization. And this is a fair and reasonable cost if your pet can be saved and perhaps even restored to health. Honest Veterinarians with old fashioned integrity will be up front with you about these issues. The purpose of this small and limited booklet is to assist you in understanding predatory veterinary practices and up-sale tactics that are becoming increasingly more common. There is an emerging mentality in many veterinary practices, that if you can't afford these extravagant prices you should not own a pet. In my humble opinion that is nonsense. Pet owners have every right to seek and demand affordable veterinary services without having to choose between providing care for their pets and paying the bills and feeding the family. In today's economy many people are working pay check to pay check and do not have an envelope with $2,000.00 to $3,000.00 set aside and marked for veterinary emergencies only.

What if after the $500.00 to $700.00 initial cost, you are informed that Gus will never be able to walk again, or will require a $5,000.00 orthopedic surgery to have a semi-normal quality of life which you simply cannot afford? Then you have to make the decision to humanely euthanize him. Wouldn't it have been better to be told that prior to all the test and X-rays which all too often are done regardless of the Veterinarian and staff knowing this would probably be the prognosis? Believe me, this is not about money, it is about kindness, empathy and understanding that not everyone can afford many of the cost thrust upon them no matter how much they love and cherish their pet. I hope to assist you in knowing what questions to ask upfront so that you don't end up a with dead dog and a repossessed car!

Old School Honesty and Integrity vs Predatory Profit Driven Policies

I do not agree that the above mentioned practices should be categorized as honest vs dishonest. However, the old school approach which I was taught and trained in the U.S. Army as a Veterinary Technician and practiced by Veterinarians with the highest moral and ethical standards is quite different from the New Age Approach that lacks complete honesty, empathy and an ability to balance the needs of the patient with the financial capabilities of loving and caring pet owners. The first and foremost difference in these two styles of Veterinary Practice starts with the Exam Fee. During normal business hours and a non-emergency practice this can typically run between $35.00 to $50.00. The exam fee for an Emergency Veterinary Hospital typically varies from $75.00 to $100.00 which is fair. But it is what you get for this exam fee that makes all the difference and you can quickly determine which type of practice you find yourself in and most importantly, demand the type of approach you can afford and that your pet deserves. First of all you should expect and receive a Differential Diagnosis as part of the exam fee. That is the Honest Old School Veterinarian will examine your pet, take an educated guess of what the problem is and if it's not a critical situation might suggest a treatment or inform you of the need for bloodwork, x-rays and/ or other diagnostic test if needed for an accurate diagnosis. A differential diagnosis is a list of different illnesses or issues that might be causing the problem based on the skills, knowledge and experience of the Veterinarian.

The Exam Fee

The initial examination by the veterinarian is where you can determine an honest, goodhearted, knowledgeable and an experienced Veterinarian who cares about you, your pet and willingness to not take advantage of your emotions and love for your pet over financial incentives. What is critical for you to understand is that you are paying this up-front fee for "His/Her Knowledge and Experience to be able to examine your pet and take a good guess what is wrong and what it takes to remedy your pet. Let's say Fifi jumped off the couch, screamed in pain and started limping, not putting weight on the rear foot. So the first thing the Veterinarian would want to know is if a bone has been broken or fractured. The honest experienced Veterinarian would get the dog excited with a piece of meat or toy and try to get him to walk without thinking about the pain. If the dog then puts weight on the leg, guess what? The leg is probably not broken or fractured! He probably would not require x-rays and then prescribe an anti-inflammatory drug, rest and see what happens. If the problem persist or gets worse, you can return and might require x-rays or other diagnostic testing. He gets his exam fee and the profit on the medication and all is well. You leave with a $100.00 to $200.00 bill, the bigger the dog the more costly the meds and you still get to pay the electric bill on time or take the kids out to eat! Compare this to the Veterinarian who right off the bat wants X-Rays, Bloodwork and Chemistry Analysis so he can read the results before even thinking about a treatment or diagnosis. Or let's take the puppy that ate the candy bar and shorty there after starts vomiting and has diarrhea. You take him to the Vet and at first you see the technician and let them know that Cujo was vomiting and had some diarrhea. A good veterinarian after checking and seeing that Cujo had all his vaccinations and seeing that Cujo has a normal temperature (100-102F), is wagging his tail, very active and readily eats a meatball out your hand might treat for indigestion and send you on your way. The cheapest parvo test is a puppy wagging his tail while being active and eating. However, once a puppy stops eating and has vomiting and has diarrhea, it is imperative to be tested for parvo and treated immediately. There is an entire section on parvo treatments, both hospitalized and my experience with in home treatments utilizing Veterinary prescribed medications and procedures.

So lets talk a little about the New Age High Tech approach of Veterinary Practices and how you can avoid the pitfalls. Unfortunately it has been my experience that far too many Veterinarians that are new to the practice are being taught not to utilize the critical thinking skills so common place in seasoned, honest Veterinarians and make no attempt to provide a differential diagnosis or suggest a treatment prior to a slew of test that after $500.00 is likely to tell them exactly what is wrong with your pet so they can prescribe the medications and treatments your pet needs.

All this information must be balanced with he fact that often your pet might require all the diagnostic test and procedures requested for an honest veterinarian to treat or save your pet and this is certainly the case with critically ill patients. The challenge is to find a Veterinarian you can trust and nothing in this book can replace the advice of a licensed honest Veterinarian. To assist you in your decision making process I have provided some of my experiences and it is my sincere hope that by sharing my experiences will provide you with the insight to make the best decision possible concerning you and your beloved pet.

True Examples of
What Not to Do

Over the weekend a male dachshund named Tank was hit by a car and is quickly taken by his emotionally devastated owner to the nearest Emergency Veterinary Clinic. Tank and his owner arrives at the Vet Clinic in a pool of blood, an eye hanging out and his back split open so much that you can see 2 of his vertebrae. He is unconscious with extensive swelling to the head and rear legs. It is a Saturday night and the owner is assured they will do everything possible to save Tank but she will need a $1,500.00 deposit for the weekend and told don't worry about the cost, you can fill out our credit application, the important thing is to treat Tank until the swelling is down enough to do surgery. The owner is a single Mother and is not given any information as to if he survives the weekend how much the surgery or surgeries will cost. She is given a written estimate for the $1,500.00 for the weekend stay. She visits Tank the next day still unconscious, cleaned up and presented in the cutest little blanket, bed and pillow by caring and loving technicians. He is hooked up to an IV drip, and the technicians are solemn and empathetic, a very touching scene that would be great for a soap opera, the only thing missing is the violin music in the background as the owner is reassured she is doing the right thing. On Monday the owner is notified that she must transfer Tank to a normal working hours veterinary hospital. He looks a little better but still unconscious and his eye is covered with moistened gauze and taped in place. As soon as Tank arrives at the local Vet she is informed that he should be euthanized as even if she can afford the $5,000.00 in surgical fees he might not ever recover as there might be permanent brain damage. She is devastated not only because of the $1,500.00 but that he was allowed to suffer the entire weekend and wished she had been advised to euthanize him on the spot minus the false hope.

An independently wealthy owner has an English Pointer named Gunther that is 14 years old and suffering from kidney failure and possible liver issues. She is about to leave town and ask that Gunther receives the best care and she doesn't care about the cost. She leaves for Europe and two days later Gunther takes a turn for the worse. He is on hormone therapy, IV fluids, tube fed and must be carried outside and messaged twice a day to urinate and defecate. He appears emaciated and obviously suffering and looking for his owner to return. Gunther's owner calls one evening while I was on duty and she ask me how is Gunther doing? As a Veterinary Technician I am supposed to say, "He is stable and receiving the best veterinary care and support possible". Instead I told her the truth, "Mam, Gunther has given you his best, 14 years of love and devotion and right now he is suffering and waiting for you to be able to say goodbye and put an end to his suffering. The word euthanasia actually means "a peaceful death". It can be the most humane final gift of love you can give to a pet that is suffering. Has anyone discussed this option with you"? She angrily replied 'Are you suggesting that I kill my dog? Let me speak to the Veterinarian now'! I got in trouble and I was counseled by the Veterinarian to never use the word euthanasia to a client unless instructed to do so by a Veterinarian. Three days later Gunther's owner came in and spent two hours with him before putting him down. In the end she made the right decision but regretted taking so long to do so.

The Veterinary Emergency Room

A Place of Extreme Vulnerability

During a life-or-death veterinary emergency we rely on the knowledge and skills of veterinary experts to provide honest and dependable information so we can decide how to proceed in a medical situation. It has been my experience that your local veterinarian, someone you and your pet has established an history and relationship with is in the best position to provide you with a fair and honest evaluation of your pets chances and possible outcomes known as a prognosis. Their input and guidance is invaluable to assist you at a time when normal decision making process simply might not apply. Finding a Veterinarian you can trust and build a relationship with is the most important step in preventing becoming a victim of greedy predatory veterinary practices.

An honest Veterinarian when presented with a chronically ill and/or advanced aged animal with little chance of recovery will not shy away from discussing euthanasia vs treatment as an option. I have seen even the most logical, calculating military commanders, stricken with grief at the potential loss of a pet. I have witnessed them being incapacitated by a sense of love and devotion mixed with guilt, being taken advantage of by emergency care veterinary professionals. Although I have seen and worked in top notch ethical emergency veterinary clinics, it is the after hour emergency vet clinics and the franchise high volume practices that the unknowing pet owner is most vulnerable. Although these clinics can provide incredible life saving procedures, it is imperative that the pet owner takes three things into consideration before they walk through the door of an Emergency Veterinary Hospital which are:

1. *I must not panic. I must maintain my control of my pets destiny and my financial obligations by making informed decisions in this emotional and financially vulnerable environment.*
2. *I must ask the right questions and evaluate the response and reactions of the veterinarian and his experienced staff.*
3. *I must consider am I keeping my pet alive and authorizing treatment for their comfort or mine? This is my decision and my responsibility to do what is best for my pet, even if it appears I am a heartless jerk for doing so.*

Now comes the hard part, when I have to tell you what the veterinary and animal care staff might not. This might be offensive to some of my colleagues but if the shoe fits, oh well! Again I need to say, there are many fine and honest veterinary clinics and staff that will give you the best advice and information that is in the best interest of your pet but for now I am going to talk about the other ones, that are not completely honest and are what I can only describe as predatory in nature. The moment you walk through the door you are a potential cash cow and the plan is to milk you for every penny they can squeeze out of you and if you can't afford it they will give you the phone to beg family members, credit applications and do whatever it takes to keep Bongo who has been hit by a car alive. The first 10 minutes when you are at your most vulnerable they pressure you to make a decision and sign an estimate, not to save Bongo, but just to know the extent of the damages if he can be saved. Please sign and pay this (Initial) estimate so we can get started on saving Bongo. If Bongo is a large dog this first initial phase might be $500.00 to $800.00 dollars, blood work, chemistries, X-rays, IV fluids, emergency drugs and emergency exam fee. In the worse state of mind you are told there might be other charges but we need your credit card and urge you to sign the estimate before we can start anything. You sign and one hour, and $650.00 later you are told that his spleen has been damaged and he needs emergency surgery so they can remove the spleen and the cost is only $3,000.00. You don't have that kind of funds and as they see your kids crying and one of them really needs a new pair of shoes you were planning on getting next payday, they tell you "no problem, here is a credit application you can fill out on your phone so we can get started ASAP". You are riddled with guilt, which for them is the gift that keeps giving. You are not sure if you can do this but the kids are crying, you love Bongo so much, he is part of the family. You are compelled to make a quick decision to save Bongo while there is still time. With a ton of guilt and sick to your stomach, you reluctantly fill out the Care Credit Application and say goodbye to Bongo as he is prepared for surgery overnight. They seem to have no concept of the vast majority of Americans that survive from payday to payday. You get a call at 3 a.m. sadly informing you that Bongo passed away and you receive a sympathy card and $3,650.00 later you are told sorry for your loss. All this seems so normal and expected in many Veterinary practices far removed from the idea and notion that an ethical and honest Veterinarian might have done the initial examination and actually noticed from palpating the abdomen and pale gums that there is a high chance of internal bleeding and that Bongo might not make it and start talking about either taking X-rays to see if surgery is an option but there is a high chance that even with surgery he might not make it. The honest, compassionate Veterinarian might even notice that one of your kids needs a pair of shoes and advise you to balance the cost vs the chances of recovery and inform you the prognosis even with surgery is not very good.

From the very beginning you have a right to ask, what will all this cost in a worst case scenario? Don't be surprised if they look at you like you are some kind of Ebenezer Scrooge, or even more common is this insane lack of empathy that suggest if you can't afford the astronomical cost of high tech Veterinary Care, you should not own a dog. Never accept the textbook response that is great for instilling a sense of guilt which is; "We don't know what the final cost might be, but the important thing is to save BONGO while we can". NO, the most important thing is that Bongo doesn't needlessly suffer and that you know up front if you can afford what the eventual cost of recovery might be. If the cost of X-rays and other diagnostic test is $600.00 and the surgical repair in addition to that is 2,600.00 and the most you can muster up in this unexpected emergency is $600.00, then as heartless as it might sound, knowing the possible outcomes and the cost of euthanasia and cremation or disposal of your pet after euthanasia might be $300.00, depending again on the size. Point being, you deserve to know all the possible outcomes and scenarios up front.

If a car salesman had it this good! The first initial treatment might be $1,500.00 and then $300.00 per day for 24 hours critical care. And although there are many clients that can afford this without the blink of an eye and if there is a chance their pet can be saved, every penny is worth it. But this information is not only for those who might not be able to afford this level of veterinary support, but also for those who can afford it but are trapped into a scenario where guilt is the driving factor and their pet suffers and then dies, regardless of the cost. The important thing is to realize that how emotionally vulnerable you and your finances might be in this environment, without the information I am so grateful to share with you, you might feel helpless. You might even feel that you, your pets life and your banking account are being taken hostage, you feel unable to take control, but take control you must and this is how.

First and foremost, pull yourself together, stop crying and take a deep breath for Bongo's sake. Take control and turn the tables simply by asking a few simple questions and closely observing the response of the veterinarian and his or her staff. These questions must be asked with eye-to-eye contact and with a look that conveys you are expecting a profound and well thought out answer. You are in a situation in which you are about to trust and give control of your pet's life and well being to the Vet and his or her staff. But more importantly, that doesn't mean you have no control over the decision making process concerning you, your pet and your checking or savings account.

In fact, it is in the best interest of all three of the above that you are able to use the information given to you to make sound, logical decisions that might affect you, your pet and your finances for years to come. You must convey that although you love Bongo and hope that he can be saved, that you are not a Cash Cow for a hopeless cause and will not allow Bongo to needlessly suffer for their profit. There are three questions you must ask. Practice them now so when or if the situation occurs you will be able to ask these with confidence and conviction that creates an expectation of truthfulness, compassion and empathy. This approach will absolutely put you in the driver seat as the decider. To accomplish this, the three question you should know by hard are these:

1. **What are the odds of Bongo's survival? I don't want him to suffer needlessly.**
2. **Am I entitled to a cost estimate for the initial treatment, next three days and euthanasia if it comes to that?**
3. **Honestly, if this was your pet what would you do?**

It is important to engage the Veterinarian more with the first question, you might want to proceed it with something like "based on your experience what is your professional opinion of the odds of Bongo's survival and restoration to a normal life"? Then you must actually ask him or her to quantify it. "Is it 50/50? Or more like 60/40 or less that he will survive and be normal? Again, I don't want him to suffer needlessly.

WOW!!!! You did it! You took control and turned the tables with just a few words! Now the Veterinarian's years of experience and professional competence is in the forefront and you must be given a real and useful answer and information to make your decision. You also let them know in no uncertain terms that you are able to make the difficult decisions and will not allow Bongo to needlessly suffer. Look At You Now! You didn't know you had it in you did you?

Am I entitled to a cost estimate for the initial treatment and the next three days?

Ok, this might be the harder question to ask. Why? Because of the psychological effect of associating a cost with the value of a life. It can be a powerful tool that if they are out to milk you for your money they can and will use against you, sometimes by simply giving you that look. You know, that simple glance of the eye? But no matter how much you love your pet, this is not a person, a child or a human life and the guilt they want you to feel simply doesn't apply. You have simply asked a question to which the answer is always an unequivocal yes. If Gonzo needs a $4,000.00 hip replacement (yes this is routinely done in dogs these days) in the next five days after the swelling has receded, which you incidentally cannot afford, why would you pay the $250.00 a day charge to keep him hospitalized, suffering in pain and strangers injecting him every few hours and prolonging the inevitable because without the surgery he will suffer and will have to be euthanized.

Honestly, if this was Your Pet, What Would You Do?

Look how far you have come! With the first two questions you have taken control of your financial obligation and liabilities while obtaining useful information and answers you need to make a good decision. All that is good and fine, however, this environment should be one of trust, honesty, compassion and empathy. Nevertheless, this can be a place of extreme emotions and vulnerability. By now it is obvious you and Bongo will not be victims, you are able to make the tough calls if necessary. But all that aside, you love your pet and you need to trust the veterinary professionals to put your pet's life in their hands. What you really need and deserve is the honesty and compassion it takes to get through a crisis such as this so you can make the best decisions.

This question, *"**Honestly, if this was your pet, what would you do**"?* cuts to the chase, and often you will be able to read on the faces of those who respond their motives as clear as day. Don't just ask the Veterinarian. The most useful feedback can sometimes be from the veterinary technicians. I assure you there are experienced Veterinary Technicians that if given the opportunity in confidence, can provide excellent advice and insights if you can win their trust. Why? Because in all honesty telling you the truth can risk their job security, so pay attention to their subliminal cues and emotional feedback. I have to laugh as I am writing this thinking about a very young couple that came in the Vet Clinic where I was working. The husband was maybe 22 and his wife was the same age or slightly younger, they had a two year old toddler in the stroller and the wife was pregnant. They rushed in crying because their cocker spaniel Sushi, had just got ran over by a car. I did the initial exam and it was obvious that this dog was not going to last the next hour no matter what we did. The Veterinarian on duty at the time was a young female, inexperienced Vet with a reputation for milking clients dry whenever the opportunity arose. But even so I fully expected her to advise euthanasia as the chances of her surviving was slim. Instead she did a 180, explaining to the young couple please sign this estimate so we can get x-rays and blood work and try to save Sushi but we need to act fast (as in please sign this before she takes her last breath any second now). I was standing behind her as she was facing the young couple face to face urging them to sign, they looked at me and I raised my hand and signaled as if I was slitting my throat and moving my head side to side and mouthing the word no. The vet turned around to look at me and thank God she didn't see what I was doing but might have suspected something. Then the couple told her, "Thank you but we don't want Sushi to suffer, can you put her to sleep"?

What Can and Should You Expect from the Animal Emergency Hospital?

So what should you expect from the veterinary services during the off hours when these events tend to occur? It depends on how critically ill your pet is. Often times when Fido doesn't seems well and it's not a real emergency, a visit to the Veterinarian can wait until the next day but a visit to the emergency vet clinic can provide the peace of mind and allow you to have a good night sleep. For example a broken nail that was bleeding but stopped, however your pet is limping but will occasionally put weight on the foot if tempted. Or a dog that over ate his food and threw up his meal but otherwise acting normal. For minor illnesses and discomforts expect to pay the exam fee close to $100.00 or a little less, and the cost of medications for treatment. Keep in mind the most likely scenario in these non-critical care situations is the technician will initially examine your pet, take temperature and other vitals. Relay his or her observations and vitals to the Vet, and then the Veterinarian will examine your pet. Remember as mentioned before, at this point you are not just paying for the Vet to examine your pet, but also for his or her opinion as to what might be wrong with your pet and what treatment options are available. Old School Vet might examine your pet and tell you what they think on the spot and offer a treatment and you are on your way. Or they might need a blood test if there is a systemic infection in which case they will typically examine and then generate a written estimate of the cost. You are entitled to question every item on the estimate and ask why this or that and what is it for?

You have every right to negotiate items on the estimate that you might not be ale to afford. Let say peanut, your male cat who had a fight with another cat a week ago is under the weather, he had a cat bite wound that ruptured and now he has an infection.

The estimate for treatment is $540.00 for the following:

$75.00 emergency exam
$200.00 Lab work blood screen
$75.00 shave, scrub clean the wound
$100.00 sedate to shave scrub and clean wound
$35.00 ointment for wound (triple neomycin antibiotic)
$55.00 oral antibiotics. Amoxi drops

There are some items on this list that you and peanut might be able to do without. For one thing the purpose of the blood test is to see if he has an infection and all signs point to the high probability that he has an infection and the treatment for the infection is the antibiotic drops for $55.00. What if you were to say, I have about $200.00 I can spend. Can we just assume he has an infection and treat that with the antibiotics and skip the testing. Peanut will allow us to keep the area clean so no need to sedate him to clean and shave. Also I just purchased a tube of antibiotic ointment, can we use that? The answers might be yes, no or a compromise. Maybe the wound must be shaved and cleaned but is it possible he can be restrained and not sedated for the procedure? That depends on his temperament and the ability of the technicians to restrain him and do the job quickly. You might have shaved a $540.00 estimate down to $130.00 exam plus oral antibiotics or even $250,00 if there is a need to shave and clean without sedation. Often if something is absolutely necessary and cannot be substituted, they will tell you and just as often these negotiations can be fruitful and productive. The important thing to know is that you have a right to ask these questions. Again, this is a noncritical scenario and not the life and death type of situations previously discussed.

The Crtical Animal Life and Death Situations

In the critical life and death situations, as we have already discussed, you must be in control by asking the correct questions and conveying the fact that you are aware that euthanasia might be the most humane outcome and have accepted that outcome if it comes to that. You must now verbalize your expectations for the following:

1. A differential diagnosis: a list of possible problems, short and log term issues.
2. A prognosis: a guess on the chances of recovery. And long term complications.
3. A cost of the initial treatment and a per day cost estimate if hospitalized.

In my 25 years of experience of working in the veterinary field, I have found that the vast majority of Veterinarians and Vet Technicians to be the most honest, compassionate and caring individuals you will find in any profession. As mentioned before, the best way to avoid predatory veterinary practices is to establish a relationship with your local normal working hours Vet Clinic. Indeed, all of my friends that live in the country and small towns have never encountered the mishaps described in this booklet. Country Veterinarians like the Amazing Dr. Po and other TV Veterinarians Dr. Russ, Dr. Blue and Dr. Lavinge of The Vets Life I hope will serve as examples of what Old School Veterinary Practices can and should be like and can inspire future to be Veterinarians what it means to care with compassion.

Unfortunately I have witnessed and resigned from clinics that have demonstrated less than honest what I can only define as predatory practices. For example, a high percentage of toy poodles will have heart murmurs, it is not atypical and almost to be expected. I remember a gentleman bringing his 4 month old toy poodle in for vaccinations and during the Veterinarian's exam he is listening to the heart and ask the gentleman, "Has your dog been coughing"? "He answered no, he is perfectly healthy" to which the Vet replied,: I *heard a heart murmur and we do have a cardiac bloodwork profile we can do for only $280.00, can I do that for you today"? The owner got really, really irritated and replied, 'I told you he is fine and I just bought him in here to get his shots". That same day another owner bought his 150 pound Rottweiler in for a spider bite lesion or small sore on his leg. He was eating fine, active and didn't have a temperature and the owner seemed very confident in knowing exactly what he wanted for his dog. And yet this very same veterinarian informed the owner he would like to do a blood chemistry to insure there were no toxins in his dog system that could have adverse effects. The owner, an obviously knowledgeable and experienced pet owner proceeded to curse the veterinarian out telling him how dare he talk to him like he is stupid and did not hold back in expressing his disgust and anger. I felt really bad for the veterinarian because he was only doing what he was being pressured to do by the clinic business management team who are neither veterinarians or mindful of delicate relationships of trust required in veterinary nursing and care.

What About Cats

Dogs think to themselves, They Love Me! They Shelter Me! They Feed Me! I Adore Them, They Must Be Gods!

Cats think to themselves, They Love Me! They Shelter Me! They Feed Me! They Adore Me! I Must Be God!!!! Cats and dogs are certainly different and so are their veterinary needs. First and foremost, cats have so many easily transmittable infectious diseases many of which are fatal. Not only should they vaccinated, but it is important that cats should also be kept indoors and not allowed to mingle with stray cats. Feline Leukemia, Feline Immune Deficiency Virus (Cat Version of HIV) and Feline Infectious Peritonitis are among the most dangerous and can easily be picked up from an encounter with a stray cat. Also, it is important that female cats be spayed and male cats be neutered early on unless you are a breeder which is not something for anyone but the most knowledgeable feline enthusiast. Therefore, when your cat is chronically ill, that is loosing weight, lethargic and just looks sick, often blood test to rule out the serious illness is often required, especially if they have been exposed to other cats. One exception which is the top killer of male cats is a blocked urinary bladder due to urinary stones. This can quickly cause death in a matter of hours. I'll never forget my first fatal encounter with this killer. I was a relatively new, inexperienced Veterinary Technician stationed in the Vet Clinic of Ft Buchannan Puerto Rico and the clinic was packed as the secretary had accidently overbooked. I got a call from a distressed cat owner asking if we could squeeze her in and I told her if she can get him here by 10 a.m. we will look at him at noon. We were so busy when he arrived I put him in a cage with a litter box and went right back to work. At noon right at the lunch break I told the Veterinarian and when we went to examine the cat he was dead. He did not look very sickly when he was bought in, he seemed rather normal to me. Then the Vet told me to feel his bladder which I did and it felt hard like a soft ball was in his stomach. He told me whenever a cat, especially a male is not feeling well, even while placing him in the cage feel the belly, if you feel a hard ball, it is a life and death emergency, a blocked bladder and we need to insert a urinary catheter immediately. I have never forgot that lesson and I hope it might serve my feline cat owners friends reading this well. This problem can occur in female cats but is much more common in males. Typically a urinalysis and x-rays might be needed to visualize the degree of stones and if that can be treated with a prescription diet, medications or might require surgery. Another problem with cats is diabetes. The cost of insulin injections, routine reading of glucose and periodic SQ fluid therapy can be significant. The quality of life of the animal and the cost of these treatments should be considered by the owner.

Emergency Treatment
for Birds

I added this section during the final stages of development for two reasons. Finding a veterinarian in time qualified to treat a sick bird can be difficult or impossible and when a bird is sickly debilitated every moment counts. The 2nd reason is as a dedication to my mentors in all things avian, Mrs. Andrea Cabibi and her recently passed husband, Phillip Cabibi PhD. Together they have saved not only countless of birds lives by offering incomparable education, training, and medical resources, but also have played a vital role in the restoration efforts of the California Condor. They have been the cutting edge of scientific avian reproductive technologies and the sudden and tragic loss of my hero Phillip Cabibi is a loss to humanity and especially to the avian exotic pet and zoological community. Andrea and Phillip Cabibi founded Taxonyx (www.cabibiscanaries.com) which can legally provide antibiotics and other medical grade medications and treatment therapies for the treatment of birds, which I have used to save sick, on deaths door step sick birds, more times than I can count.

Critical Emergency Intervention for bird species requires an understanding and appreciation of their extremely high metabolism and the need for immediate treatment in the form of heat/warm and immediate administration of calories to sustain life. Typically the smaller the bird the faster the metabolism and the less time you have to save the bird. I have been amazed at the speed in which a finch or canary found on the bottom of the cage can recover enough to begin medication treatment after providing warmth in the form of a heat lamp (not too close as to cause heat stress) with the administration of a high calorie electrolyte solution. I mixed 1 cc of Honey with 9 cc of Pedialyte Solution and using a 1 cc syringe slowly give a few drop at a time can mean the difference between life and death. You can make your own electrolyte solution if you obtain the powdered packets from any Feed Store known as SAVACHICK packets. Warmth and Electrolytes is only the first step in restoring the metabolic resources necessary to sustain life. When birds are deathly ill they crash quickly and truth is there may be nothing you can do to prevent death. If one of my finches was sick at night, I knew I would find them dead my morning if not treated. If you can find and afford a veterinarian willing to treat exotics, by all means do so. Please understand the intervention of heat, calories and electrolytes is simply the first step of emergency intervention, the nest step is to figure out why they are sick? Is it dehydration from lack of clean water? Is it bacterial from dirty water or food/ Fungal infection or a virus? Andrea Cabibi has written two books on the treatment of sick birds that any person who owns exotic and typically expensive birds should absolutely own or anyone who owns a bird they care dearly about should arm themselves with the knowledge and resources to treat them if they are inclined to do so. Again the best resource I know of is Taxonyx and these items can be ordered on line at www.cabibiscanaries.com I have found the most common source of sicknesses to be bacterial infections and after administering first aid as described, carefully mixing antibiotics with an oatmeal type of chick feeding powder such as Kaytee Exact as prescribed can sometimes quickly in a manner of days restore a sick bird back to health. Another common danger to avian health, especially in an aviary is dehydration. In hot weather if water temperature is too hot to drink it is the same as not having any water at all. I have used water bottles from feed stores for baby chicks with excellent results. I would freeze them overnight and place them in the aviary or cages once the temperature got too hot and this has saved many lives from heat exhaustion. Also, I have to admit these resources I had on hand for my birds served me well when I had to pull an entire litter of puppies through parvo by having the antibiotics on hand once I got them to hold food down. Just a word to the wise.

Can Veterinary Business Models Be Condusive to Depression and Suicide?

I was not going to include this section, however, during the final editing of this booklet a story was shared on KTLA Channel 5 News Los Angeles discussing the abnormally high rates of depression and suicide of Veterinarians. There is very little debate or research addressing the root cause of the high rates of depression and suicide in the Veterinary Care Field and I feel I have touched upon it from the perspective of the Pet Owner but that is not addressing the toll that the Profit First Veterinary Business Model is taking on perhaps the most innocent victims, which are Veterinarians. Veterinarians have devoted most of their lives, perhaps even from childhood to helping animals, healing the sick and ministering to "All Creatures Great and Small". Typically compassion and empathy is the very core of their soul, it's not just what they do as much as it is who they are. To achieve this they go to years of college, a very demanding educational marathon in which, unlike human doctors they must learn everything there is to know about multiple species and multiple disciplines. They are surgeons, radiologist, family practice, pediatrician, pathologist, and so on and so on all rolled up in one. And after obtaining this incredible accomplishment and earning a Doctors Degree in Veterinary Medicine upon graduation they enter the workforce fully expecting to utilize their skills to helping not only the animals, but their grateful owners, including the least of these my brothers. The family of six, with four kids and the dog they love, that is hurt and critically needs the skills and God given talents of the Veterinarian. Some of these new Veterinarians will find practices that will allow them to fulfill their life's calling, but far too many will land their first job in a Veterinary Franchise or something similar in which the business model allows them to examine the patient, talk to the owners but do not allow them to treat the animal unless that owner or family can afford what might be a probative cost. When this person, male or female, is faced with this scenario several times a day, day after day, family after family, I believe it takes a mental toll. I have seen it firsthand. The pressure put on Veterinarians to generate very high estimates for treatments and often the only other option is euthanasia. Imagine this constant dilemma, sorry but if you don't have 2,000.00 I cannot help you and I suggest to put Fiona down, being faced several times a day, day after day by someone who's very soul is one of compassion and empathy. It can become unbearable. I know several Veterinarians that have taken less lucrative positions in order to do what they love for those who have the least. Working in Low Cost Vaccine Clinics or Humane Society Low Cost Spay and Clinic Programs, even if it's one day a week. It is a day they can give back to the community and fulfill the calling on their lives. I sincerely believe this is a powerful factor in the high incidents of depression and suicide in Veterinarians, so if or when you are faced in these high pressure sale situations, realize it might very well be the business model of the institution. Often, as suggested, if you ask the question, "What would you do if this was your animal"? can circumvent the situation.

I almost got fired one time for refusing to tell a young couple that their puppy had parvo when I knew he did not. In fact I did not even know why the Vet would order a parvo test on a puppy that is wagging it's tail and eating food out the hand but he insisted because he had diarrhea ordered a parvo test. Anyway, I ran the test and it was negative as the control spot turned blue but the positive control was clear, however there were some discoloration along the edge of the test but no where near the positive control. The supervisor looking over my shoulder said, oh, you can call that test positive and I replied no I can't because that is a negative result, she called the veterinarian over and he agreed with the supervisor it was positive. As a Certified Lab Animal Technologist very familiar with these test I told them, I cannot lie to these people and that test is negative to my knowledge, I was told to leave early for insubordination and they went in and told that young couple that the test was positive and they should either euthanize him or allow treatment and hospitalization for $2,000.00. I later learned they chose to euthanize the puppy and I was heartbroken. Had I known this was going to happen, I would have gone in that treatment room and told them everything, tell them to inform the Vet, you can't afford to treat but will take the puppy home, even at the risk of being fired. It wouldn't be the first or the last.

Hydrogen Peroxide and Poisoning

Disclaimer: In case your animal is poisoned, the best advise is to get them immediate veterinary treatment as soon as possible whenever feasible. However, if you are an hour away from a veterinary facility, hydrogen peroxide, might save your pet's life.

We were moving from San Bernardino, California to Apple Valley, California and we had several family members with their dogs and ours over, everyone working together to pack and load the moving trucks and the garage was wide open. There was my daughters white German Shepherd, Elsa, my Decker Hunting Terrier Ariel and her puppy Rags as well as her other puppy that was visiting Decker. In horror I noticed all four coming out the garage with three of them with the bright green granules that is unmistakably rat poison blocks they must have found that I was unaware of was in the garage! I immediately gave all dogs 1 cc of hydrogen peroxide per pound. So Elsa got 50 cc and the terriers got from 15 to 20 cc each. After 5 mins I gave Elsa a 2nd dose and in 3 mins she started vomiting and clearly vomited up the chunks of green rat poison. She kept vomiting until the vomit was clear fluid which convinced me all the poison was out. At the same time the other three were vomiting two of which had some small amounts of the rat poison and the third did not. Hydrogen Peroxide can be used to induce vomiting providing that the substance swallowed is non caustic, like acid or bleach or something that will burn the lining of the esophagus coming back up. It can be effective if given immediately after ingestion and before it has a chance to be absorbed. Nevertheless, in the case of poisoning, poison control should be called (800) 222-1222, and veterinary advice should always be followed.

Prevailing Over Parvo

No discussion concerning Veterinary Care can be complete without addressing the issue of Parvo disease, the enormous cost of treatment and the critical importance of prevention. The most important information I can share is undoubtably steps to prevent parvo which is Vaccinating the dam shortly prior to her being bred, vaccinating the puppies with veterinary temperature-controlled vaccines, preferably from a veterinary clinic. The reason I say this is because vaccines purchased from a feed store might or might not have been kept at the critical temperature from shipping to being placed in the refrigerator of the feed store.

Also, I have been told that there are some veterinary policies that guarantee the effectiveness of parvo vaccines if done through the veterinary clinic. Another important prevention is keeping visitors away from newborn and pre-weaned puppies. I know how tempting it is to have a litter of puppies born, accepting deposits from potential buyers, and having customers arrive to see your beautiful litter. But the possibility of having people track the parvo virus into your home and resulting in the death of the entire litter is not worth the risk. Also, there is a critical time that the maternal anti-bodies from the mother and the anti-bodies from a vaccine can cancel each other out. So the age between 5 and 6 week old puppies for me is the most critical. For a litter of puppies, vaccines can be ordered on-line. I have found Neo-par to be the most effective in protecting puppies against parvo virus and can be ordered on-line and delivered to your door on ice. It can be purchased in 10 dose vials which I would give at 5- 6 weeks, 8 weeks of age and then every 3 weeks until 16 weeks old which would be done by the new owners. It is one thing to have a beloved puppy contract parvo and having to deal with the typical $2,000.00 treatment. Having a litter of puppies is an altogether different monster I will address and discuss to treat in house.

First and foremost, the best and most effective treatment for a dog or puppy with parvo disease is the intense treatment they can receive in a veterinary hospital where they can receive 24 hours of intravenous treatment, antibiotics and drugs that can reduce and cease the constant vomiting and diarrhea. A puppy or dog can die of parvo in two or three days and the primary cause of death being dehydration, the loss of fluids from the vomiting and diarrhea and the inability to orally replace the fluids lost due to vomiting and diarrhea. That is why IV fluids and medications delivered directly into the veins or intravenously is so effective. If you have a puppy that stops eating, begins to vomit and has diarrhea, parvo can and should be the primary cause for concern and must be treated immediately. The typical cost of an average size puppy is $2,000.00 for a three day stay at the Veterinary Hospital. However, the larger the dog or puppy, the higher the cost because the various prices of medications and treatments is typically based on the weight of the animal. And even though the preferred treatment for parvo disease is hospitalization, it is possible, with the help and support of a Veterinarian that has examined and diagnosed your puppy for parvo, to treat your puppy at home. I had a litter of 11 Decker Hunting Terriers that came down with parvo, even after being vaccinated and lost 2 puppies early on before I could get my hands on effective treatments which I administered at home. But once I started, I pulled the remaining 9 through, some of which were so sick they could not even stand to their feet and were totally emaciated from being unable to eat for almost a week. Perhaps pulling this litter through the worst case of parvo, although exceedingly difficult and challenging, it might turn out to be a blessing to others at risk of losing an entire litter to this dreadful disease. I thank God I had the help and support of so many people, including one of the puppies future owners Carol Pike, the owner of Legendry's Ain't Misbehaving (aka Jazz). More information concerning this battle against parvo and photos can be viewed on my Face-Book Page VET TECH ARMY STYLE or deckerhutningterrierbook Facebook Page.

As mentioned, parvo puppies and dogs can be treated at home with the assistance of a Veterinarian that has examined the dog and diagnosed it as positive for parvo disease. The reason this is critical is because the Veterinarian is legally required to examine and diagnose parvo in order to prescribe the medications you need to take home and treat parvo disease. This is where the critical difference between Old School Veterinary Practices and New Age The Need For Greed Profit Above Compassion is really where the rubber hits the road. During my dilemma of a parvo positive litter of pups, I could not find a Veterinarian willing to do what I desperately needed but I did find one that was willing to compromise. The Vet examined the four puppies that were the first to get sick, I paid an examine fee for each pup which was $35.00 each, one was tested for parvo (35.00 for the test) and when that came back as positive, he could assume all four were positive. That was a compromise in itself as New School Practice might insist that all four be tested to be able to prescribed medications for all four. Home treatment was a feasible option for three reasons, I absolutely didn't have $8,000.00 to treat four puppies being hospitalized, The Vet Clinic didn't have the available resources to house and treat four parvo puppies at once as they were already treating three puppies at the time which require isolation from other pets, and being a retired U.S. Army Veterinary Technician, they knew I had the skills to administer the medications which I will hope to share here and on my Face-Book Page VET TECH ARMY STYLE which has photos that are very helpful. If I were to include photographs in this booklet it would significantly increase the cost and my vision is to make this booklet so affordable that every pet owner will want to have and will want other pet owners to have, perhaps as a gift.

Once diagnosed, the veterinarian was able to provide me with the initial treatments, which consist of three critical elements: 1. I.V. Bag of 0.9% Sodium Chloride or 0.9% NaCl. 2. Injectable medications in the form of a cocktail or combination of injectable medications that can be administered SQ which means subcutaneously or under the skin and 3. Anti-vomiting medications such as sucralfate to coat the stomach similar to Kao-pectate.

1. The Sodium Chloride or 0.9% is a bag of fluid that an IV line is inserted and butterfly needle can be attached to to the other end of the IV line so that fluids can be administered under the skin or subcutaneous fluid therapy. This is the first and most critical step of keeping the puppy alive. The needle is placed under the skin in between the shoulders or withers as fluid flows and forms a large bulge of fluid. Instructions on administering subcutaneous fluids is readily available on VCA Animal Hospital websites. The amount given varies on the weight and size of the dog. My puppies weighed about 5 to 7 pounds and got from 50 to 100 mls per treatment. A decent guideline for me is that the bulge can be about the same size as the head and given whenever there is indication of dehydration. To

test for dehydration and the extent of dehydration simply pull the skin up over the shoulders and the speed and degree in which the skin snaps back into place indicates the degree of dehydration. If the skin snaps back into place no treatment is needed. If it slowly returns to place the animal is dehydrated and might need treatment but if it fails to drop back or doesn't return completely and looks more like a tent, the animal is severely dehydrated and needs immediate fluid therapy.

2. SQ Injectable Medications. Each Veterinarian will have his or her preferred cocktail but typically it will be a combinations of injectable anti-biotic such as Baytril or enterfloxlin, Reglan or metoclopramide, Vitamin B12 Vitamin Complex and dexamethasone, an anti inflammatory steroid. I purchased a 100 ml premixed cocktail of the above injectables as follows

   a. 5 mls of Regulan
   b. 30 mls of Vitamin B12
   c. 15 mls of dexamethasone
   d. 10 mls of Baytril
   e. 40 mls of 0.9% NaCl

   Total 100 mls and the Vet prescribed 3 cc per pup twice a day.

3. Sucralfate suspension acts similar to pepto bismol and kao-pectate for people in as much as it coats the stomach and helps prevent vomiting. In addition the sucralfate also slows down stomach motility that can help with both vomiting and diarrhea. The problem with parvo dogs is that they vomit everything up,

but it might stay down if given in small amounts. A much better anti-vomiting drug that bypasses the digestive track is **Zofran or Odansetron** which a small amount of 0.1 to 0.3 mls can be applied under the tongue 0n a 5-10 pound puppy and this will help prevent vomiting.

These injectable medications and drugs, the dosage and concentrations must be prescribed by a veterinarian and given as directed. Again, each Veterinarian will have their own formula if they are willing to do this at all. If this is the only way an entire litter can be treated and saved, I would hope you will be able to find a veterinarian to sell and then prescribe the treatments so that that after initially purchasing the SQ fluids and anti-vomiting meds you can order on line from either Farm Vet or Revival Veterinary Supply. These medications are critical for the first three days with the goal being to wean them off these expensive prescribed medications onto more affordable home treatments once they are able to keep down fluids such as vitamin enriched broth and eventually an oatmeal consistency food with anti-biotics such as Baytril or Amoxicillin. The 100 ml bottle of cocktail mixture was $80.00 per bottle and with 9 parvo positive puppies I went through 1 bottle every three days and used three bottles before they improved enough to wean them on less expensive therapies. During the worse battles I would get up every three hours and find 2 or three puppies that would not survive the night without SQ fluids and at times my Lazarus Elixir which can bring a puppy on deaths door step the energy they need to stay alive while you are administering the slightly warm SQ fluids saved several pups. Lazarus Elixir is a quick way to replenish electrolytes and sugars the brain needs immediately and is simply a mixture of Pedialyte 8cc, 2 cc of karo syrup 2 cc of beef or chicken broth. This can only be given 3 cc as any more is likely to be vomited up. If the ondansetran is available place a few drops under the tongue to give that prior to trying to administer the elixir. I purchased beef bones and pressure cooked them and used the broth as a first food. I followed this with a Gerber baby food type of baby foods like chicken which came in a 50 ml bottle to which I added 500 mg of amoxicillin to have 10 mg per cc dose of baby food medication and fed each pup 10 cc twice a day once they were able to keep food down. Once they were able to keep food down they are on the road to recovery. Everything being based on the knowledge that dehydration is the main killer with parvo and getting them from SQ fluid therapy to being able to keep water and broth down and using Pedialyte to battle the dehydration and antibiotics to fight the secondary infections was critical. Nevertheless, I thank God for giving me the strength and skills to pull these puppies through and the support of friends and future owners. There were some who wanted their deposit back and others who were such a blessing from God and so grateful for their pups once they were restored to health. If you have to deal with parvo, DO NOT SKIP THE SECTION ON EMERGENCY BIRD TREATMENT. As these resources can be useful.

The Final Gift

The decision to have your pet put to sleep is yours and yours alone. It may very well be the greatest gift of love an owner can give to a pet who has given a life-time of love and devotion without ever asking for anything in return except food, shelter and companionship. It can be and often is the most difficult and heart wrenching decision anyone has ever made. It is my hope that this booklet will provide you with the knowledge and conviction to make an informed decision. The right decision that can provide you and your pet the peace and serenity you both deserve at a time when love, devotion and what's in the best interest of your pet and the animal emergency hospital staff may very well be at odds.

WHAT ABOUT EUTHANASIA?

For Your Comfort or Theirs's

Perhaps one of the most difficult decisions and acts of love any pet owner can do is to have the strength and to know when to let go. Death, even that of your beloved pet is a natural part of the life process and all too often we use veterinary advances to prolong the inevitable death and thus the needless suffering of our pet. Today more places are offering professional veterinarians to come to your home and perform the procedure in a warm heartfelt comfort zone for the pet and their owner. The question we must ask is this: are we avoiding euthanasia which means a peaceful death for our sake or what is the most humane thing for a suffering pet?

Understanding The Grief From The Loss of a Pet

There are people who have never loved and lost a pet and will never understand the heart wrenching grief some people experience at the loss of a beloved pet. They simply do not understand and may say or think something like "get over it, it was an animal, not a child". Some people will think you are overreacting and simply cannot comprehend the pain, emptiness and depression that can occur from the loss of a pet. What they fail to see and understand is that many of us are closer to our pet than members of our extended family. We see them every day. They depend on us daily for food, shelter and companionship. They don't hold a grudge when we fail them and are always happy to see us when we come home as if they have won the lottery. We love them and they unconditionally love us back. To have that unconditional love and routine suddenly removed from our lives can be traumatic and lead to depression for good reason which they might never understand. Although your pet can never be replaced, it might be a good thing to allow another furry friend that needs your capacity to love and care as much as you can use something to occupy that empty place in your heart. I sincerely hope this booklet has helped you and if so I urge you to share it with others. I also invite you to check out my Facebook Page Vet Tech Army Style and soon to be released book

VET TECH ARMY STYLE, Adventures in Veterinary and Animal Sciences in the United States Army by George W. Heath BS, LATG

Printed in the United States
by Baker & Taylor Publisher Services